SMALL-SCALE SOAPMAKING

To Fiifi and Araba

SMALL-SCALE SOAPMAKING

A handbook

Peter Donkor

Technology Consultancy Centre, University of Science and Technology, Kumasi, Ghana *in association with* IT Publications

Intermediate Technology Publications Ltd., 103-105 Southampton
Row, London WC1B 4HH, UK.

ISBN 0 946688 37 0

Printed by the Russell Press Ltd., Radford Mill, Norton Street,
Nottingham NG7 3HN, UK.

Contents

Preface

In April and May 1985, I visited Ghana to gather data for a book on the work of the Technology Consultancy Centre at Kumasi's University of Science and Technology. TCC was founded in 1972, in an effort to adapt and transfer to ordinary Ghanaians some of the knowledge that is often held captive within university walls. It was soon discovered, however, that the *development* of appropriate technologies was not the same thing as the *transfer* of technology, and it became clear that the Centre would have to involve itself not only in projects that were relevant to the cultural and economic environment of the community, it would have to become involved in the community itself. This, in turn, led to an appreciation that even a basic technology like soapmaking cannot be compartmentalized. Thus, making soap became a bit like pulling a thread on a shirt: if you pull long enough, you will find that it is connected to half the universe.

Making soap in the context of Ghana's protracted economic difficulties meant not only the development of a simple method that could meet rural conditions, but one that could survive the temperament of the wildly fluctuating market place as well. When caustic soda, an essential ingredient, became unavailable, TCC devized a technique and equipment for local manufacture. The traditional method of extracting oil from the palm fruit is laborious and expensive, and so in order to reduce costs and the burden on the women who do the work, TCC developed a low-cost oil press, the production of which is now firmly established in several small workshops in Kumasi. When palm oil became almost totally unavailable during the drought and the economic crisis of 1983, TCC began a search for non-edible oil substitutes, conducting successful experiments with both neem and castor oil. Perfume was developed from lemon grass. A measure of the success of such experiments is the recent adoption of some of TCC's techniques and findings by the large Lever Brothers soap plant in Accra.

Peter Donkor's book modestly avoids discussion of the great pains that he and others put into the development of the technology he describes, and of the success that has been achieved in having the process adopted on a widespread scale in Ghana, by small urban and rural entrepreneurs, by village co-operatives and by development organizations. A further measure of success has been the number of requests from other countries in Africa for assistance in establishing the process. Peter Donkor has travelled to Guinea Bissau, Mali, Togo, Sierra Leone and Mozambique to help set up small soapmaking enterprises. He is therefore uniquely equipped to write about a process which has been tried and tested, not only in the sterile laboratories of the Ghana Standards Board, but in the bustling shops and stalls of the Ghanaian market place.

Ian Smillie
London, 1986

Acknowledgements

There is no doubt about the fact that a lot of people have contributed in one way or another to the success of this book.

My special thanks go to Dr. J.W. Powell, Director of TCC, whose encouragement and editing as well as contact with the Intermediate Technology Publications made the publication of this book possible. My sincere thanks also go to the Intermediate Technology Development Group in the UK, for funding the printing of the first edition of this book.

I will also like to express my heartfelt thanks to the following people and companies: Miss Esther Akom and her assistants Miss Grace Dery and Angelina Pamford, all of TCC, who typed the draft of this book, Mr. W.A. Osekre, the University photographer who printed some of the pictures used in the book, the Obegam Soap Enterprise, Kumasi, and Kwamotech Ltd, Kwamo, who allowed some pictures of their workshops to be taken for this book.

Last and not the least, my special gratitude goes to Mr. Smillie who agreed to write the preface of this book. Mr. Smillie paid a visit to TCC (when this book was being written) to write up a comprehensive report on the activities of the Centre.

Note

Further information about equipment such as that mentioned in Chapter 4 can be obtained by writing to the Technology Consultancy Centre, Kumasi, Ghana.

Chapter 1

Introduction

1.1 Brief History of Soapmaking

The need for soap, a cleansing agent, has been felt ever since man became aware of the necessity to clean his body and environment in the primitive ages. Soap has therefore acquired the status of a basic necessity in the modern civilized world. Soapmaking is one of the oldest industries in the world; most authorities claim that it originated on the sacrificial altars of early primitive people, when fat from animals killed on altars dripped over wood ashes, thereby combining with the potash in the ashes to form crude soap.

1.1.1 The Development of Soapmaking in Europe

It is recorded that the Gauls were the first to produce soap by mixing goat fat (tallow) with potash from beechwood ashes, and were followed by the Romans who learnt the art after the conquest of the Gauls, under Julius Caesar. Soap manufacture seemed to flourish in the eighth century in Spain and Italy, and was introduced in France some 500 years later, when factories were established in Marseilles for soap manufacture from olive oil. In the fourteenth and fifteenth centuries, soap was manufactured on a commercial scale in Italy in the city of Savona, and the words "savon", "sabon" and "jabon", which are French, Portuguese and Spanish words respectively for soap, are derived from the name of the city.

The first record of soapmaking in England is in 1552, and from this time to the beginning of the 19th century, manufacture of soap developed very slowly, being carried on essentially by the rule-of-thumb method. In 1787 and the years that followed, a major breakthrough was made in soap production as a result of two discoveries. Nicholas Leblanc discovered a process for the chemical production of caustic soda from common salt in 1787, and a few years later Michael Eugene Chevreul carried out a successful research into the constitution of fats and oils, and demonstrated that soapmaking was a chemical process involving the initial splitting of fatty acids and glycerol. These findings gave the soapmaker an unlimited supply of one of his basic raw materials — caustic soda. They also placed the soap industry on a scientific basis as soapmakers were now in a position to know the nature of the chemical reaction involved in soapmaking.

The history of many modern soapmaking companies in England can be traced back to the eighteenth and nineteenth centuries, although their growth at the time was hampered by high taxation. However, following the scientific breakthrough, soap taxation was abolished in England, resulting in the rise of the demand and supply for soap. During this period, W.G. Lever became a dominating figure in the soap trade in England. In 1884, he introduced sunlight soap for the first time. Gradually, other soap manufacturers began developing different kinds of soap for cleaning different articles, and more attention was also given to the form in which the soap was presented. Lux flakes, for example, were first marketed in 1900, and were a big success. Lever also introduced the use of tropical vegetable fats and oils like palm oil, coconut oil, palm kernel oil, etc, for the making of soap at a time when the traditional sources of animal fats for soapmaking were running behind demand in England.

1.1.2 The Development of Soapmaking in Ghana
Soapmaking was an indigenous technology in the country long before the arrival of the Portuguese in 1482, especially among the Fanti tribe who were making soap from crude palm oil and potash from wood ashes. Though this potash soap is still being made and used in the rural areas of Ghana, very little improvement has been made on the processing method to produce a good quality soap acceptable to the urban soap consumers. Probably the rural population still enjoys the use of this soap for bathing purposes because of its good cosmetic properties. Though the soap is very soft and usually black or

2

ash colour, it is very mild and has some bleaching property on the skin, which has made the use of the soap very popular among women who prefer to be fair in complexion. Apart from its bleaching property, it is also used for dermatological purposes. Its use in the treatment for ringworm, and prickle heat rashes is well known.

The sort of nature of potash soap, and its short-shelf life coupled with the difficulty in the preparation of caustic potash (prepared from the ashes of cocoa pods, plaintain peels, etc) and/or the scarcity of potash at the local market, has limited the production of this soap to some extent. It was no surprise that when the country was colonized the indigenous soapmakers swiftly switched over from the production of the traditional soap to the laundry soap introduced by the colonial masters, which involved the use of ready-made imported caustic soda.

1.1.3 Large-scale Soap Production in Ghana
Since the first Portuguese stepped on the shores of the land, laundry soapmaking has steadily been carried out on a small scale by local soapmakers along with the dwindling volume of potassium soap production. In 1963, Lever Brothers set up a soap complex in Tema to start large-scale production of laundry, toilet and powder soaps to boost the local production of soap. More recently, two other soap complexes have been established in Kumasi and Cape Coast.

1.1.4 The Role of Research Institutions in Ghana
One interesting situation with the local production of soap in the country is that very little attempt has been made to improve on the quality of soap produced. It is unfortunate that up till now all sorts of low quality soaps popularly known as 'Don't touch me', because of their high caustic soda content and slippery nature, are produced in the country.

Although some research programmes have been carried out to improve the quality of soap by the research institutions, their findings have not benefited the small-scale traditional soapmakers who produce both the laundry and potash soaps. The biggest attempt yet made was by the Technology Consultancy Centre (TCC) which in 1983 set up a pilot soap plant to conduct research on the improvement of local soaps and to offer free training to local soapmakers on the technology of good quality soap production. The Centre still offers this training and produces soapmaking equipment for sale to local soapmakers.

The Centre's current soap training programme is geared towards the production of laundry soap but some attempts are also being made to improve the colour and hardness of the traditional potash soap.

1.2 Definition of Properties

The definition of soap is generally restricted to the combination of fatty acids and alkalis obtained by reacting various animal and vegetable fats and oils with caustic soda or potash, the former giving hard soap and the latter soft soap.

Both soaps are readily soluble in hot water or alcohol. However, they dissolve very slowly in cold water forming a turbid solution owing to slight decomposition. Sodium soaps (made from caustic soda) are found to be insoluble in very strong caustic solutions, and for the most part in strong solutions of brine; hence the addition of strong solutions of brine to a solution of sodium soap causes the soap to separate out and rise to the surface of the caustic or salt solution. This separation (also referred to as 'graining') of soap is employed in commercial soap production. On the other hand, addition of brine to a solution of potassium (potash) soap merely results in double decomposition giving rise to sodium soap and potassium chloride.

Thus $C_{17}H_{35}COOK + NACl = C_{17}H_{35}COONa + KCl$
i.e. (Potassium Soap) + (Common Salt) = (Sodium Soap) + (Potassium Chloride)

The solubility of different soaps in brine varies very considerably.

1.3 Hydrolysis of Soap

When soap is treated with cold water it is said to undergo hydrolysis — the breaking down of the soap into its component parts. The hydrolysis results in the liberation of an acid salt. The reaction can be represented in its simplest form by the equation:

4

$$2 \, C_{17} \, H_{35} \, COONa + H_2O = NaOH + HNa \, (C_{17}H_{35} \, COO)_2$$
(Soap)+(Water)=(Caustic Soda)+(Acid Salt)

1.4 Detergent Action

Many theories have been proposed to explain the detergent action of soap — the property possessed by soap to remove dirt. However, the commonest explanation is that the alkali liberated in the process of hydrolysis attacks any greasy matter on the surface being cleansed, and as fat is dissolved, the particles of dirt are loosened and easily washed off.

Another theory suggests that the alkali set free by the hydrolysis of soap serves as a lubricant, making dirt less adhesive, and thus promoting its removal.

Yet another theory states that the alkali tends to lower the surface tension of the water, and thus permits the emulsification of fat-bearing dirt particles on the surface of the material being cleansed.

Chapter 2

Raw Materials for Soapmaking

The raw materials for the making of soap cover a wide range of substances which may be classified under the following headings:
1. Fat and oils
2. Alkalis
3. Filling agents
4. Water
5. Salt
6. Perfumes
7. Colours or dyes

However, fats and oils constitute approximately 90% of the soapmaker's raw materials, and a detailed treatment of fats and oils is made in this chapter.

2.1 Fats and Oils

The cost of production and properties of any particular soap are largely dependent on the nature and properties of the various oils and fats used in its manufacture. Thus it is very important for the soapmaker to be fully conversant with the physical, chemical and soapmaking properties of the oils and fats being used. Since no two oils have identical soapmaking properties, the art of soapmaking lies not only in the boiling operation but in the judicious selection of the oils and fats to produce the qualities needed.

2.1.1. Classification of Fats and Oils

Fats and oils are esters of fatty acids and glycerol. The distinction between fats and oils is purely an arbitrary one, based on their physical state at ordinary temperatures — the

6

oils being liquid and the fats solid or pasty.

Fats and oils are divided into three classes, namely, fixed oils, mineral oils and essential oils. However, fixed oils form the main raw materials for soapmaking as they decompose into fatty acids and glycerol when strongly heated, and are easily saponified by alkali. Fixed oils and fats, which include both animal and vegetable fats and oils, are further classified according to their physical properties as follows:

a) *Nut oils:* These oils are characterized by a large proportion of fatty acids with low molecular weight, especialy lauric acid. Examples of these oils are coconut oil and palm kernel oil. These oils (especially coconut oil),when used in toilet soaps are the chief suds-producing ingredients.

They saponify easily with strong alkali solution (30-35°Bé). Once these oils begin to saponify the process proceeds rapidly with the evolution of heat. They also require large quantities of strong brine (16-18°Bé) to grain their soaps, and the grained soaps tend to carry more salt than other soaps. These oils are more suitable for the making of cold process soaps.

b) *Hard Fats:* The hard fats contain appreciable quantities of palmatic and stearic acids. Examples of these fats are palm oil, animal tallow and hydrogenated oils. These oils or fats produce slow-lathering soaps but the lather produced is more stable over long periods of time than the nut oils. In soapmaking, they are first saponified with weak alkali (10-15°Bé), and in the final stages with stronger alkali solutions.

c) *Soft Oils:* These oils have substantial amounts of unsaturated acids, namely oleic, linoleic and linoleneic acids. The soapmaking properties of these oils vary with their fatty acid composition, and the physical and chemical properties of the acids. Examples of these oils are groundnut, castor, cotton seed, fish oil and olive oil. These oils cannot produce hard soap when used alone for soapmaking. They are usually blended with nut oils. Their soaps, however, lather freely and have very good detergent properties.

2.1.2 Brief Chemistry of Fats and Oils
Soapmaking involves a definite chemical decomposition of fats and oils into their constituent parts, namely fatty acids and glycerol. The fatty acids combine with caustic soda, potash or other base to form soap, and the glycerol remains free.

Plate 1: Oil palm tree

8

All fats and oils used in soapmaking consist of a mixture of compounds of glycerol with fatty acid which occur in nature in the form of triglycerides. The most important of these acids from the soapmaker's point of view are stearin, palmitin, olein and laurin. The presence of stearin and palmitin, which are solids at room temperature, gives firmness to fats and oils. The greater the percentage present the harder the oil or fat, and the higher its melting point. Where olein, which is liquid at ordinary temperature, is the chief constituent, the oil or fat is soft.

The soapmaking properties of fats and oils can be determined by the molecular weights of their fatty acids. With increasing molecular weight in the case of naturally occurring saturated fatty acids in fat or oil, the following properties are found:

1. The boiling point of the oil rises,
2. The melting point of the oil/fat rises,
3. The saponification value of the oil/fat decreases.

Also, the properties of their corresponding sodium soaps vary as follows with increasing molecular weight:

1. The solubility increases,
2. The lathering properties improve up to lauric acid and deteriorate from lauric acid upwards,

Plate 2: Palm kernels

9

3. The stability of the lather increases,
4. The detergent action decreases,
5. The soaps have milder skin action as the series progresses,
6. The property of holding filling solutions such as sodium silicate decreases.

This explains the reason why nut oil (such as coconut oil) soaps lather readily and profusely but not stably. They also have a firm texture and are hard but dissolve more readily in water than do soaps from the hard oils. They can also retain a good amount of water, and take up fairly large quantities of fillers like sodium carbonate.

Naturally occurring saturated fatty acids
(The $C_nH_{2n}O_2$ Series)

Common Name	No. of Carbonisations	Chemical Formula	Molecular Weight	Melting Point (°C)	Occurs In
Butyric	4	C_3H_7COOH	88.1	− 8	Milk fat
Caproic	6	$C_5H_{11}COOH$	116.16	− 2	Milk fat
Caprylic	8	$C_7H_{15}COOH$	144.21	16.0	Milk fat
Capric	10	$C_9H_{19}COOH$	172.26	31.3	Coconut
Lauric	12	$C_{11}H_{23}COOH$	200.31	43.6	Coconut
Myristic	14	$C_{13}H_{27}COOH$	228.37	54.0	Animal fat
Palmitic	16	$C_{15}H_{31}COOH$	256.42	63.0	Animal/ vegetable fat
Stearic	18	$C_{17}H_{35}COOH$	284.47	69.6	Animal/ vegetable fat
Arachidic	20	$C_{19}H_{39}COOH$	312.52	75.3	Groundnut
Behenic	22	$C_{21}H_{43}COOH$	340.57	80.0	Groundnut
Lignoceric	24	$C_{23}H_{47}COOH$	396.67	85.87	Beeswax

2.1.3 Common Oils used in Ghana for Soapmaking

Various oils and fats have become established in Ghana for soapmaking. These are all edible oils, although some attempts have been carried out by the TCC to identify local non-edible oils as substitutes for edible oils for soapmaking.

These oils which are extracted locally using both commercial and traditional technologies include palm oil, coconut oil, palm kernel oil, shea butter and cotton seed oil.

1. Palm Oil
Palm oil is extracted locally at the commercial level using

10

Plate 3: Coconut tree

11

hydraulic presses, and at the small-scale level using hand-operated screw presses.[1] However, traditional extraction techniques cater for about 30% of the total palm oil produced in the country. The oil forms about 50-60% of the total oils and fats used in Ghana for soapmaking.

Palm oil usually produces a crumbling soap which canot be readily milled for toilet soap production, but with 20-25% coconut oil blend, it produces satisfactory toilet soap.

ii. Coconut oil

The oil is produced from copra mostly in the Western Region, by the Esiama vegetable oil mill, using oil expellers. However, traditional extraction methods are used widely in the Western Region and other areas of southern Ghana. The oil is extensively used to blend other oils like shea butter, palm oil and cotton seed oil for soapmaking because of its property to produce hard and lathering soaps. It also finds application in the production of liquid soaps because its potassium soap remains clear at low temperatures.

Because of its high saponification number, it requires a strong caustic solution (known as lye) for its saponification. Its soap is usually white, firm and soluble with rapid forming lather which is not very stable.

iii. Palm Kernel Oil

This oil is produced mostly in Ghana using traditional techniques and is used interchangeably with coconut oil in both laundry and traditional potassium soapmaking. Its soap has similar properties to coconut oil soap.

iv. Shea Butter

Shea butter is a fat which is extracted in the northern part of Ghana, where shea trees are found, using only traditional extraction techniques. The fat is somewhat tough and sticky, and the amount of unsaponifiable matter present is considerable.

The fat produces soap of soft consistency with oily appearance and thus needs to be blended with coconut or palm kernel oil to improve the hardness and lathering properties. It

1. This technology was developed and promoted by the TCC. A full account of the technology can be found in the TCC report 'The Development of Appropriate Technology hand screw press for the extraction of palm oil' by Peter Donkor.

12

is the chief fat used in the north for soapmaking, since most of the other oils mentioned are not found in the north.

v. Cotton Seed Oil

Cotton seed oil is not widely produced in Ghana. The Crystal Oil Company in Accra is the main producer of cotton seed oil soap stock for soapmaking.

The crude oil saponifies with ease but the soap is difficult to grain. It produces soap of soft consistency, if used alone, and has a bad odour.

2.2 Alkalis

The two alkalis popularly used in the making of soaps are caustic soda and caustic potash.

2.2.1 Caustic Soda

Commercial caustic soda is creamy in appearance and fibrous in structure. It readily absorbs moisture and carbonic acid from the air to form sodium carbonate. Due to its hygroscopic property of absorbing moisture, it must not be exposed to the air. Caustic soda is also very corrosive to the skin and aluminium containers, and as such must be handled with great care. It is available on the market in various forms, namely flakes, powder, sticks and blocks. The powder and the flakes are very convenient to handle but are costlier than the solid or block caustic soda, and are normally used when the volume of soap production is very small. For large soap production units, however, it is more economical to buy solid caustic soda in drums. To remove the caustic from the drum, the drum is first pounded on all sides with a heavy iron hammer, causing the caustic soda to crack. The cracked caustic is then chiselled and broken into pieces and dissolved in the right amount of water to obtain the concentration needed.

Commercial Production

Commercially, caustic soda is produced by the electrolysis of brine (sea water), the byproduct of such a process being chlorine which is used for bleaching and water treatment. The description of the process involved in caustic soda manufacture is beyond the scope of this book and will therefore not be discussed.

PLATE 4: *Using hydrometer to determine the strength of caustic soda solution.*

Local Production (Using Precipitation Reaction)

In Ghana, the Technology Consusltancy Centre (TCC) of the University of Science and Technology (UST), Kumasi, has developed a technology for the local production of caustic soda. The technology which was designed to produce 100kg of caustic soda of about 80kg in 9-10% solution and 20kg in 5% solution has generated a lot of interest amongst small-scale soapmakers, and the government which is currently promoting the technology among the members of the Ghana Soapmakers' Association.

2.2.2 Description of process for local production

Raw materials

The raw materials required for the making of the caustic soda are:

a) sodium carbonate — an imported raw material bought from

ICI (Ghana) Ltd., Tema, or the open market in 50kg bags;
b) slaked lime — a by-product of the manufacture of acetylene from calcium carbide and water by L'Air Liquide. Presently, the lime is a waste material for the company, and is collected by soapmakers free of charge.

Equipment:

The equipment for the manufacture of the chemical is a cylindrical tank reactor (Plate 5) made from galvanized steel sheet with a diameter and height of 120cm (4ft). The reactor is equipped with four baffles which extend from top to bottom at 90° to the walls of the tank. Their purpose is to promote a good agitation of the slaked lime suspension during the reaction. An agitator, axially positioned in the tank, consists of a shaft and a 4-bladed axial flow turbine which is 17·5cm (7in) above the bottom of the reactor. The width of each blade is 4cm (1·6in), the length is 16·05cm (6·42in), and the pitch of the blade is 45°.The shaft of the agitator is directly rotated by a 1hp electric motor at a rotational speed of 950rpm. The agitator and the baffles have been designed to keep the lime in suspension during the reaction.

45cm (18in) from the bottom of the tank, along the walls of the reactor is a swivelling decanting pipe with 31.25mm (1¼in) valve through which the clear solution of caustic soda is decanted, and at the centre of the bottom of the reactor is a 10cm (4in) valve through which the sludge of calcium carbonate (a byproduct of the reaction) and unreacted lime is discharged after rinsing with water.

The reactor can be wood fired, or electrically heated with five domestic heating elements each of 2kW rating. The designed production capacity per day is 100kg of caustic soda, and has a design reaction temperature of 90°C and reaction time of three hours.

Process

Nine hundred litres of water is measured into the reactor and heated to a temperature of 92-95°C. Using the heating elements, this temperature is attained after about eight hours' heating, but with strong firewood, it takes only about three hours. When the temperature is reached, the agitator is

15

PLATE 5: Caustic soda plant.

switched on, and 150kg of sodium carbonate introduced into the water for absolute dissolution. When the carbonate is completely dissolved 182kg of dry slaked lime is introduced into the reactor, and the reaction allowed to take place for three hours to completion with continuous agitation. After three hours, the heating is stopped and the calcium carbonate suspension is then allowed to settle after which the clear solution of 10% caustic soda is decanted. The 5% weaker solution is then obtained through the agitation (or washing) of the calcium carbonate with about 300-400 litres of water, before the calcium carbonate is drained out. When used for soap-making, this carbonate goes into the soap as a filler.

2.2.3 Caustic Potash

Caustic potash possesses chemical properties similar to those of caustic soda. It is, however, much stronger in chemical reaction than soda. It produces soap of soft consistency and higher solubility in water than sodium soaps, and is therefore generally used for the making of liquid soaps, shampoos and soft soaps.

Commercial Production

Commercial production of caustic potash involves the same two methods as already described in the production of caustic soda, namely precipitation reaction method and the electrolysis method.

In the precipitation reaction, slaked lime is reacted with potassium carbonate, while in the electrolysis method the electrolyte used is potassium chloride.

Local Production

In Ghana, caustic potash is produced on a small scale by traditional soapmakers from a number of vegetable ashes. The process is described as follows:

Raw Materials

Cocoa pods, spent palm bunches, plantain or banana peels, kapok tree wood.

Equipments

Basket or earthenware pot, jute bag or straw, tray or bucket, wide and shallow pan to crystallize caustic solution.

2.2.4 Description of Process for Local Production

The process involves burning any one of the raw materials mentioned above into white ashes. It must be noted that the raw material must be very dry before being burnt at high temperature to ensure complete combustion and the production of fine white ashes. A kiln has been designed by the Engineering Faculty of the University of Science and Technology (UST) for the production of white ashes. Some of these kilns are being used in the southern part of Ghana for the production of white ashes for caustic potash manufacture.

Plate 6: UST-designed kiln for wood ash production

After burning the raw material, a given volume of the ashes is measured into a big basket lined with a clean jute bag, and placed on a drum by means of two horizontal rods. The ashes are moulded up around the sides of the basket to leave a depression in the centre to ensure proper draining of the caustic solution. An earthenware pot with a small hole made at the bottom can be used as a substitute for the basket.

A quantity of warm water (about twice the volume of the ashes put in the basket) is slowly added to the ashes, allowing

18

the ashes to absorb as much water as possible before adding more water. After the ashes have absorbed enough water, brown lye (caustic potash solution) begins to drop slowly from the bottom of the basket into the tray or drum under it, as more water is put on the ashes. The dripping must be slow enough to allow maximum dissolution of the caustic potash in the ashes in the water put in the basket. When no more solution drops, the lye obtained is put back in the basket to repeat the leaching process. This second leaching increases the strength of the lye.

A suitable strength for soapmaking can be checked crudely by dipping a chicken feather or putting a fresh egg into the solution. A stronger solution will dissolve the feather, or support an egg. A hydrometer can also be used to determine the density of the solution, if available. If the solution is found to be weak, boiling will concentrate the solution to the required strength.

2.3 Other Raw Materials

In addition to fats, oils and alkalis, a lot of other chemicals are used in comparatively small quantities to give various characteristics to soaps. These chemicals include builders, fillers and various other additives.

Builders
Building agents are essentially used to 'build up', i.e. increase the detergent power of soaps. Their use in soaps has enabled the soap industry to face, to some degree, the severe competition from synthetic detergents. Sodium carbonate, sodium silicate and sodium sulphate are alkali builders commonly used in soapmaking.

Fillers
Fillers are used to add weight to the soap without in any way adding to the detergent property of the soap. They increase the bulk of the soap, and hence reduce production cost. They are not, however, used in good quality genuine soaps.

A number of filling agents are used as fillers, but the most popular ones are clay, kaolin, talc, starch, common salt, chalk and magnesium carbonate. Soda ash and sodium silicate are also used in large quantities as fillers — sodium silicate when used, also acts as an antioxidant to protect the soap from going rancid. It also improves the smoothness, binding, transparency and hardness of the soap. In the use of fillers, care must be taken for their selection and quality as too much may dampen the washing properties and keeping quality of the soap.

Common Salt
Brine (a saturated solution of salt) is very important in soap manufacture. It is needed to grain out the soap in a full boiled process, in order to separate out glycerin and excess caustic from the genuine soap. Salt used in graining has to be pure, i.e. free from compounds of iron (Fe), calcium (Ca) and magnesium (Mg), otherwise they will cause the deterioration of the soap and introduce impurity in the form of their insoluble soaps.

Colours
Colour is added to soap to make it more attractive, and sometimes to mask the original colour of the product. Oil and water soluble dyes are suitable for soap colouring.

Perfumes
Some oils and fats produce soaps of unpleasant odour (even if they are well clarified before use) which need to be perfumed. However, in the use of these perfumes, consideration must be given to the action of the particular perfume on the soap. Some synthetic perfumes and essential oils cause soap to darken rapidly on keeping, e.g. clove oil, and vanillin, while others decompose the soap. Lemon grass oil, citronella oil, oil of lavender (French) and bergamot oil are suitable oils.

Perfumes are added to soaps at low temperatures as they are very volatile at high temperatures.

Chapter 3

The Choice of Suitable Oils and Fats for Soapmaking

Whether soap production is done on a small or large scale, the quality and properties of the soap to be produced depend to a large extent on the type of oil used; hence the choice of a suitable oil is very necessary for the production of good soap. Many small-scale soapmakers in Ghana seem to be ignorant of this important fact, and therefore produce soaps of poor quality. Though a lot of technical and economic factors determine the choice of oil by the soapmaker, e.g. availability of the particular oil needed, and the type of equipment and machinery as well as the process of manufacture being used, certain specific constants of the oil or fat determine the hardness, lathering properties and washing efficiency of the soap to be produced. Knowledge of these constants, if used properly, is a big asset to the soapmaker. They help to forecast the quality of soap to be expected from the choice of a particular oil or blend of oils used.

The most important of these constants are the Saponification Value, Iodine Number, the INS Factor and the Solubility Ratio (SR). This chapter briefly describes the meaning of these constants and their applications to soapmaking.

1. Saponification Value

This very important constant helps to determine the quantity of caustic soda or potash required to neutralize (saponify) a given quantity of oil or fat chosen for the making of soap.

It is defined as the quantity of caustic potash (in milligrams) required to saponify 1g of oil or fat. Saponification values are always expressed in terms of caustic potash. Therefore the

21

value if given must always be multiplied by a factor (0·7) to obtain its value in terms of caustic soda.

Let us see the practical use of this value in soapmaking, by assuming that a soapmaker has 3kg of palm oil for soapmaking, and he is told that the saponification value of the oil is 202. How can he estimate the quantity of caustic soda required to saponify the oil? This can be worked out as follows:

If the saponification value of the oil is 202, then the quantity of caustic soda required to saponify 1g of the oil is 202×0.7mg (ie $202 \times 0.7 \times 10^{-3}$g). Hence the quantity of caustic soda required to saponify 3000g (3kg) of the oil will be $202 \times 0.7 \times 10^{-3} \times 3000$g, or 424·2g. Thus from the given saponification value, the soapmaker knows that he requires 424g of caustic soda to process the 3kg of oil into soap.

Saponification Value and Iodine Numbers for Some Common Soapmaking Oils and Fats

Oil/Fat	Saponification Value*	Iodine number
Palm Oil	200-205	49-59
Coconut Oil	251-264	8-10
Palm Kernel Oil	248	11-15
Shea Butter	178-189	56-65
Cotton Seed Oil	193-195	108-110
Animal Tallow	190-199	35-46
Vegetable Tallow	192-195	40
Lard	195	59-63
Neem	186-204	69.0
Groundnut	186-194	90-103
Sunflower	189-194	126
Castor	181	84.1

*These values represent the number of milligrams (mg) of 100% caustic potash required to saponify 1g of the oil. In order to calculate the amount of caustic soda required we must compare the relative molecular weight of caustic soda (40) and caustic potash (56).

$\therefore$ Caustic soda required $= \frac{40}{56} \times$ saponification value/g of oil

$= 0.7 \times$ saponification value/g of oil

Let us consider this second example by assuming that a soapmaker has a blend of oil consisting of 1kg of palm kernel oil and 3kg of palm oil for soapmaking, given that the saponification values of the kernel and palm oils are respectively 248 and 202. Let us determine the quantity of caustic soda required to saponify the 1kg (1000g) of kernel oil.

22

Since it has a saponfication value of 248, the quantity of soda required will be $248 \times 0.7 \times 10^{-3} \times 1000$g, i.e. 173·6g. That for the 3kg palm oil is found to be 424·2g. Therefore 598g of caustic soda will be needed to saponify an oil blend of 3kg palm oil and 1kg palm kernel oil.

It must be noted, however, that the saponification value is of significance while making soap using the cold or semi-boiling process, but in the full boiling process it is of little or no significance since any strength of caustic soda solution can be used and grained. The average saponification value for most of the soapmaking oils (excluding the nut oils) is 190.

3.2 Iodine Number

This constant is defined as the number of centigrams of iodine absorbed by 1g sample of the oil. The number, in fact, indicates the presence of unsaturated acids in the oil or fat. The higher the number for an oil, the greater the percentage of these acids, and thus the softer the soap produced from the oil. The soft oils (like cotton seed oil and groundnut oil) have high iodine numbers and are readily oxidized. The iodine number thus indicates the hardness of the soap, the lower the number, the harder the soap produced. Cotton seed oil has an iodine number of 109 while coconut oil has an iodine number of 9. This explains why coconut oil produces hard soaps.

The use of this number in determining the hardness of soap produced from a blend of oils is not very reliable since it does not give any information on the nature of the unsaturated acids in the blend. The saponification value, on the other hand, gives directly the molecular weights of the fatty acids in the blend, and thus indicates the presence of lower molecular weight saturated acids. In view of this it is very advisable to make use of the two constants in the selection of the suitable oil for a particular soap to be produced. This gives rise to another factor known as the INS (Iodine Number Saponification) factor.

3.3 INS Factor

This factor is expressed as the difference between the iodine number and the saponification value of the oil or fat. It is used to predict the quality of soap to be obtained from a blend of oils. This factor ranges from 15 to 250 for soapmaking oils and fats. The liquid oils with high proportions of unsaturated fatty acids have low factors while the hard fats and nut oils with low molecular weight saturated acids have high factors.

Generally, with increasing INS factor, the following observations are found:

1. the oils vary from liquid to solid and produce harder soap;
2. the detergent and lathering properties as well as the solubility of the soap decreases (except the nut oils) with improved colour, and capability to hold more filling agents;
3. the soap or oil diminishes in its tendency to go rancid on ageing.

INS Factors of Common Oils and Fats used in Soapmaking

Name of Oil/Fat	INS Factor
Coconut Oil	250
Palm Kernel Oil	235
Vegetable tallow (mafura)	165
Mutton tallow	155
Beef tallow	150
Palm Oil	146
Lard	137
Olive Oil	108
Cotton Seed Oil	85
Soya Bean Oil	54
Linseed Oil	15

3.3.1 Practical Application of INS Factor

According to the Ghana standards for soap, a good soap should have the following physical properties:

1. good colour, bright in appearance, and free from objectionable odour;
2. be of medium hard consistency, and produce free and stable lather over long periods of time.

The above standards indicate that oils with extreme high and low INS factors are both unsuitable for use alone to make soap, as the nut oils with high factors will produce too hard a soap and the soft oils with lower factors will produce too soft a soap. The hard oils with medium factors (e.g. palm oil and tallow) will be the best. They, however, produce soaps of low lathering power, and must therefore be blended with soluble and quick lathering oils or fat with lower INS factors. These oils on the other hand have the dual purpose of increasing the lathering properties of the soap as well as softening the soap, the degree of softening depending on the quantity used for the blend. It is therefore necessary to increase the hardness by adding a certain proportion of a nut oil (e.g. coconut oil) to the blend. This will further increase the lathering properties of the soap. Therefore a good oil blend must be made up of a nut oil (coconut oil), soft oil (ground nut oil) and hard oil (palm oil).

It is interesting to note that the nut oils are unique oils for blends since they have the property of increasing both hardness and solubility of soaps while all other oils capable of hardening soap (e.g. tallow, palm oil) have the disadvantage of reducing solubility.

The question now confronting the soapmaker is: what quantities of these three oils (soft oil, hard oil and nut oil) should be suitable for a good oil blend to produce the required quality of soap?

Let us consider how the INS factor can be used practically to resolve this issue.

Let us assume that a soapmaker has to make a blend of palm oil, coconut oil and cotton seed oil such that the blend will have an INS factor of 146 (which corresponds to that of palm oil and lies in the INS range for soap oils) and constitute 50% of palm oil. We therefore need to determine the percentages of cotton seed oil (say, X) and coconut oil (50−X) which must be added to the palm oil to form the blend.

Using the INS factors of the oils, we add up these factors according to their percentages present in the blend, and the sum should be equal to the INS factor of the blend, i.e. 146.

Therefore, for palm oil: $\frac{50}{100} \times (146)$

for coconut oil $\frac{(50-X)}{100} \times 250$ and for cotton seed oil $\frac{85X}{100}$

$$\therefore \quad \frac{50}{100}(146) + \frac{250}{100}(50-X) + \frac{85X}{100} = 146$$

i.e. X = 31.5 and (50−X) = 18.5

Thus the blend should consist of 50% palm oil, 31·5% cotton seed oil and 18·5% coconut oil

The above calculations may seem a little cumbersome to a

lot of local soapmakers but if followed carefully they help the soapmaker to form a suitable blend, with the quantities of oils at his disposal, since a blend of the same INS factor produces soap of the same hardness irrespective of the component parts of the blend.

Lathering and Solubility Properties of Soap

The lathering and solubility properties of soap is found to be dependent on the INS factor of the oil or oil blend used in the making of the soap. Oils and fat with an INS of 130-160 are individually unsuitable for soapmaking on account of low lathering. Though the low INS factor oils reduces the hardness of soap, they tend to increase the solubility, but the rate of softening is greater than the rate of solubility increase. Thus the presence of coconut or palm kernel oil (high INS oils) in these soaps are essential since they have marked effect on both hardness and solubility.

However, the following observations must be noted as the use of some of these oils is subject to limitations:

a) Palm kernel oil, which serves as a good substitute for coconut oil in soapmaking, should not be used in toilet soaps as the odour of the oil is likely to develop in the soap with time. Also any oils with high levels of unsaturated fatty acids (cotton seed oil) are not suitable for toilet soapmaking on the grounds of rancidity.

b) Generally, any quality of tallow, and bleached palm oil can be used to make household laundry soaps, where colour plays an important role. Among the soft oils, cotton seed oil is most preferable for a blend, but sunflower and soya bean oils are the best substitutes for cotton seed oil.

c) It is worth noting that, although current choice of an oil or fat is very important, it is only a necessary but not a sufficient condition in good soapmaking. Improper processing techniques during the soap saponification process will produce a low quality soap in spite of the choice of suitable oils.

Chapter 4

Plant and Equipment for Soapmaking

Plant and equipment required for small-scale soap production units vary in design from one place to another. Generally, they include soap-boiling pans for soap boiling, wooden or metal soap frames to hold liquid soap for solidification, a cutting table to cut solid soap blocks into slabs, bars and tablets, a foot or hand operated stamping machine, hydrometers to measure the strength of caustic soda and common salt solutions. Caustic soda mixing tanks, and other items like rubber gloves, weighing scales, buckets, and polythene sheets for frame lining.

4.1 Equipment and Plant for Laundry Soapmaking

4.1.1 Soap-boiling Tanks

These pans may vary in size and material depending on the maximum volume of soap to be boiled and the process being used, but they are normally made of mild steel or cast iron or galvanized materials of suitable gauge. Generally, the pan has a cylindrical body with a truncated conical base (to effect easy drainage of the hot soap), and a drainage pipe fitted to the bottom of the pan.

A typical wood-fired boiling tank designed by the TCC and popularly used in Ghana by small-scale soapmakers is made of 16 gauge galvanized steel in the form of a cylinder measuring 121cm in diameter and 90cm in height welded to a truncated conical base of 30cm high and 30cm in bottom diameter (Plate 7). The total volume of the boiling tank is 1600 litres and it is capable of boiling half a tonne of soap per batch. At the bottom of the tank is a 3cm hole fitted with a 3cm galvanized

Plate 7: TCC soap-boiling tank

28

steel pipe with a matching gate valve through which the boiled soap is discharged into the soap frames. The tank is mounted on a one metre high ring frame support, made of 2.5cm iron rod, surrounded by burnt bricks and clay with an entrance and a chimney to form a hearth for firewood heating.

In some developing countries like India, the wood-fired boiling tanks are gradually being replaced by tanks equipped with closed and open coils through which steam at about 45psi flows (from a boiler) for the boiling of the soap.

In the rural areas of Ghana, soapmaking at the village level is done using a 200 litre oil drum for the boiling of the soap.

4.1.2 Caustic Soda Storage Tanks

This is a tank in which caustic soda solution of the required strength is prepared and stored for use when needed. The tank may be rectangular or cylindrical in shape, but made of a strong and thick material to withstand attack from caustic soda.

4.1.3 Soap Moulding Boxes

These are wooden or metal frames into which the boiled soap is run for cooling. The boxes are rectangular in shape and the number of boxes used by a soapmaker depends on the volume of soap normally produced in the unit. The sides of the frames can be made to be taken apart for easy removal of the dried soap, or can be permanently nailed. If the latter is used polythene sheets are used to line the box before the boiled soap is run into them.

A wooden soap moulding box designed to give 52 bars of soap of $3.7 \times 6 \times 37$cm in dimensions will measure $20 \times 4 \times 96$cm inside with a wall thickness of 2cm.

4.1.4 Soap Cutting Tables

After the soap is hardened and taken from the soap moulding box, it is in the form of a solid rectangular block which needs to be slabbed and further cut into bars or tablets as required. This is done using a cutting table (Plate 8). The wooden table is four or six legged, with a cross bar running width-wise across its central line, and boards 9cm high running length-wise along each side. On one side of the table along the cross bar are two or three suspension wires kept taut by a butterfly nut on top of the cross bar. The gap between any two wires is arranged to

Plate 8: Soap-cutting table

30

give the dimensions of the soap slab when cut. Similar sets of suspension wires are arranged on the other side of the table to cut the slabs into bars or tablets.

The soap block is cut into slabs by manually pushing the block against the suspension wires.

4.1.5 Stamping Machines

To give a commercial finish to the cut soap tablet, the soap is moulded into a precise shape and an inscription or trademark of the manufacturer put on one or both surfaces of the soap using a stamping machine. The foot or hand operated machine has a vertical treadle motion and gives a direct blow to the soap. Two dies are normally required for both surfaces of the soap are stamped. The dies are made of hard brass for a better finish. The bottom die normally rests in the box which holds the soap while the top die is fixed to the plunger. To stamp the tablet, it is put in the soap holder and the hand or foot lever operated. The two dies, with the trademark engravings on them, move vertically in opposite directions against the soap, which is thus stamped on both sides. The stamped soap is automatically released on the return stroke.

4.2 Plant and Equipment for Small-scale Toilet Soapmaking

The preparation of toilet soap on a small-scale involves various operations of soap base preparation, chipping of soap base, mixing of chips with perfume and colour, milling of soap into flakes, compressing of milled soap, and cutting and stamping of compressed soap.

Equipment required for the preparation of the soap base, cutting and stamping of soap tablets is the same as already described under Section 4.1. However the mixing, milling and compression operations require the following equipment.

4.2.1 Mixing Machines

This is also called an amalgamator and is used to mix the dry soap base (in the form of chips), perfume, colour and any other additive. The unit consists of a hopper fixed on a mixing drum provided with a tilting arrangement for easy unloading of the mixed material (Plate 9). The mixing is done by a sweep of blades made of stainless steel. The Indian model designed for

31

use by village and cottage soap industries has a material handling capacity of 20kg/hour.

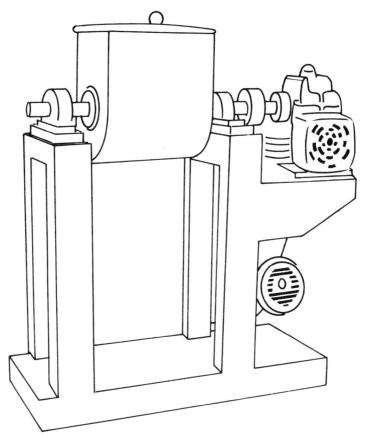

Plate 9: Mixing machine

4.2.2 Milling Machines

The object of milling is to render the soap more homogeneous. The milling machine consists of a hopper sitting on a chamber of three or four granite rollers fitted with a suitable gearing system (Plate 10). The rollers are connected in such a manner that they rotate at different speeds, thus increasing the efficiency of the milling process, and ensuring that the action of the rollers is one of rubbing rather than crushing. By means of suitably arranged screws, the pressure of the rollers on one another can be adjusted to give the issuing soap ribbons any required thickness.

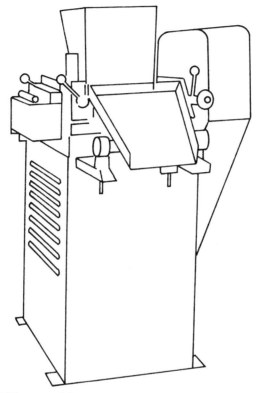

Plate 10: Milling machine

4.2.3 Plodders
The plodder, also called an extruder, is a compressing machine which compresses and binds the milled soap ribbons into a solid bar suitable for cutting and stamping. It consists of a hopper set onto a strong metal conical-shaped cannon-like tube which tapers towards the nozzle, and in which a single or twin screw is moving and propelling the soap to the conical end (Plate 11). When the soap is fed into the compression chamber, it is forced through a perforated metallic disc, and subjected to high pressure to be compressed. The soap finally

emerges through the nozzle to which an attached cutter of suitable shape cuts the extruding polished and neat soap bar into the required length. The nozzle is equipped with a cartridge electric heater providing temperatures between 50-55°C to allow the soap to be easily forced out. The temperature is automatically controlled through a thermostat provided at the top of the heating chamber to avoid the soap becoming blistered if the nozzle is too hot, or being of poor and dull appearance if the temperature is low.

The Indian model has a material handling capacity of 20kg/hour.

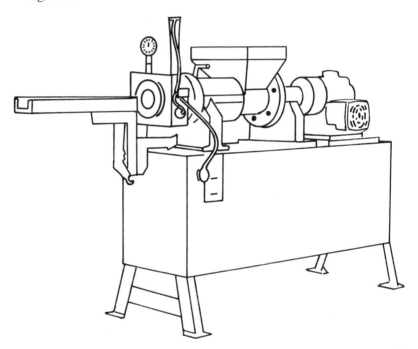

Plate 11: Plodder

4.3 Other Equipment and Tools

Apart from the plants and equipments described in this Chapter, certain useful items are also required in the general art of soapmaking. These items include a weighing scale for weighing raw materials; rubber gloves and boots to prevent bodily contact with caustic soda solutions; enamelled, galvanized or plastic buckets or containers to hold caustic soda solution, water and oil; a plastic sheet for lining the soap moulding box; and a stirrer if stirring soap is to be done manually during the boiling process.

Chapter 5

Pre-Treatment of Fats and Oils for Soapmaking

In Chaper 3 the raw materials required for the making of soap were discussed. Notable among these materials are fats and oils. Depending on the characteristics of the fats or oils they may be subjected to various pre-treatments like clarifying, bleaching and deodorizing. The sort of treatment to be applied depends on the oil type and its purity, as well as the type of soap to be produced with the oil.

5.1 Refining of Oils and Fats

Oil refining comprises various processes of clarification of oils and fats to rid them of impurities and free fatty acids, and any unwanted odour, and the bleaching of the oil to remove objectionable colour.

5.1.1 Alkali Refining

Irrespective of the process used in the extraction of oils, the crude oil may contain certain amounts of objectionable impurities which may consist of pulp, and other components of the oil seeds or nuts in suspension. Also, during periods of storage and handling of the oil seeds, slight decomposition (gradual breakdown of the glycerides) of the oils in the seeds usually occurs giving rise to the presence of free fatty acids in the oils, the extent of the decomposition depending on the length of storage of seeds. The presence of free fatty acids, water and other impurities are chiefly responsible for the rancidity of oils, thus making saponification of the oil very difficult.

One of the common methods used in the refining of oils and fats is by the use of weak caustic solution, referred to as alkali refining. During the process, the free fatty acids in the oil react with the weak caustic soda solution to form soap stock which also absorbs some colour, odour and impurities from the oil, thus rendering the oil clean.

It is always advisable to determine, as a first step in the refining process, the content of free fatty acids in the oil sample (by titrating the oil with standard alkali) to enable the soapmaker to calculate the amount of caustic soda required for the refining. For example, if it is found that the free fatty acids present in an oil sample is $0 \cdot 6\%$, then 100kg of the oil contains $0 \cdot 6$kg of free fatty acids to be neutralized. A 20°Bé solution (of relative density $1 \cdot 16$) of caustic soda is normally used for refining. Such a solution contains $14 \cdot 3\%$ of pure caustic soda. It is also known that 14% (by weight of fatty acid) of pure caustic soda is required to neutralize a given weight of fatty acid.

Thus $0 \cdot 6 \times 0 \cdot 14$kg, or $0 \cdot 084$kg of 100% caustic soda will be required to refine 100kg of the oil. Using a 20°Bé solution (of 14.3% strength) $0 \cdot 084/0 \cdot 143$ or $0 \cdot 59$kg of the solution will be required to refine 100kg of the oil. In practice, however, $0 \cdot 1$-$0 \cdot 5\%$ more solution is used.

The process of alkali refining involves heating the oil in a suitable tank to around 32°C, and while stirring the correct quantity of 20°Bé caustic solution is evenly sprinkled on the surface. After several minutes of the addition of the solution, brownish or dark clots, which are saponified acids and gelatinous impurities, will be formed in the oil while it is being stirred. The oil is then heated to 50°C and the stirring stopped. It is then allowed to cool overnight, after which the refined oil is siphoned through a swinging draw-off pipe.

5.1.2 Another Clarification Method
A simple method of clarifying oil at small-scale and cottage soap industries in Ghana involves boiling the oil or fat in half its volume of water for 4-6 hours. Some scenting materials like lemon grass, cinnamon leaves, orange peels, etc, are added to the boiling oil. During the boiling process the steam from the oil-water mixture takes along with it some of the undesirable odour of the oil while the scenting materials give some scent (deodorize) to the oil. After the boiling, the fire is put out and the mixture allowed to cool. The clean clarified oil which floats

37

on the top of the water is then siphoned from the tank while the water with the settled impurities from the oil is drained off from the bottom of the tank.

5.1.3 Bleaching of Oils and Fats

Three bleaching methods are generally employed in the bleaching of oils and fats, namely earth bleaching, air bleaching and chemical bleaching.

Earth Bleaching

In this process the clarified oil to be bleached is heated to 90-100°C, and 4% of Fuller's Earth and a small quantity of activated charcoal are added to the oil and slowly agitated for 15-20 minutes to keep the bleach in suspension. The oil and bleach are then filtered in a filter press, or the oil is allowed to cool for a night and decanted, when the bleaching agents settle down to the bottom of the tank.

Air Bleaching

This process is widely used in rural soapmaking for the bleaching of palm oil. In this process, clarified palm oil is heated to 200-250°C in an open tank for 4-6 hours depending on the quantity of oil treated. In the course of the heating the oil is oxidized and the red colour of the oil soon vanishes. In some cases where the bleaching is done in a steam jacketed tank with an open (perforated) coil, air is blown continuously through the oil by means of the coil when the oil is heated to 100°C.

Chemical Bleaching

This process is generally used for the bleaching of palm oil and other deep colour oils like cotton seed oil and mustard oil. The method, which is referred to as the bichromate method, involves dissolving potassium bichromate in hot water and adding the solution obtained to the clarified clean oil heated to 52°C. Dilute sulphuric acid is then run into the oil and stirred well. The bright red colour of the oil gradually changes into a green colour, and after some minutes of agitation, the oil is allowed to cool and the green chrome liquor at the bottom of the tank on which the bleached oil floats is drained off. The oil is then washed (without further heating) with hot water containing some common salt to remove any traces of chrome liquor left. For every tonne of oil 10-12kg of potassium bichromate and 20-27kg of dilute sulphuric acid is used. Care must be taken so that the bleaching temperature of 52°C of the oil is not exceeded or else the resultant oil on saponification will yield a soap of reddish-brown colour.

Chapter 6

The Processes of Soapmaking

Various attempts have been made to produce soap by first decomposing the fat or oil into fatty acids and glycerin, and then converting the acids into soap by treatment with sodium or potassium carbonate. However, three conventional methods of soapmaking are generally used in both large- and small-scale soap production units. These methods include semi-boiling, full-boiling and cold processes, and will be discussed in this chapter.

6.1 Semi-boiling Process

The process, although not suitable for the production of toilet soaps, can be used to produce laundry and all types of soft and liquid soaps. The process does not permit the removal of waste lye which contains the glycerin produced in the soapmaking process, and hence the glycerin, which tends to decrease the hardening property of the soap but improves the cosmetic property, is retained in the finished soap. However, the method has some advantage over the other two since large quantities of good soap can be produced within a short time. The use of the method also allows a high percentage of fillers to be incorporated in soaps, thus increasing the soap bulk. In Ghana about 70% of the laundry soap and all the traditional potassium soaps produced by the small-scale producers employ the semi-boiling process.

6.1.1 Processing Method

The soft and hard oils or their blends are very suitable for this process which involves melting the oil or fat and running a weak 9-10% caustic soda solution into the oil, and boiling the mixture. In all 14-15% of the weight of the oil is the quantity of

40

caustic soda required for the saponification of the oil. This weight of caustic soda is dissolved in ten times its weight of water to obtain a 9% solution. When the caustic solution is run into the oil, saponification starts when an emulsion is formed as the soap is stirred. More caustic solution is then run in to prevent the mass thickening. After sufficient solution is added bit by bit to complete the saponification, boiling of the mass continues until the soap is clear.

During the boiling process moderate heat is maintained and each addition of caustic soda solution must be allowed to react with the oil before the next addition is made. A hasty addition of the lye in the initial stages of the process may retard the saponification, or at the final stages of the saponification may result in the graining of the soap, while judicious addition will keep the mass in a form of smooth homogeneous emulsion. If the soap shows any signs of separation or graining, further water or oil is added to bring the mass to a homogeneous state.

Plate 12: Weighing caustic soda with a spring balance

The end of the process is easily recognized by an experienced soapmaker. However, crude tests can be made to determine when saponification is completed. The 'ribbon test' involves taking a small sample of the soap from the pan and cooling it. When a little quantity of the cooled soap is pressed between the thumb and forefinger, the soap should come out in the form of firm shiny ribbons with slight opaque ends and be clear when held against the light. If the cooled sample draws out in threads, there is an excess water present in the soap, and further boiling is required to evaporate more water. If the opaque ends appear and vanish, the soap is oily and requires more caustic, while if the soap is grainy, or turbid and somewhat white, it indicates a high level of unreacted caustic, and requires more oil. A physical test — the taste test — can also be done to determine the level of caustic. This test involves cooling a small quantity of the soap, and tasting with the tip of the tongue. A very sharp bite indicates too much caustic in the soap, while no bite at all indicates a high level of unsaponified fat or oil. A good soap should give a faint bite on the tongue.

After the completion of the boiling process, the fire is withdrawn, and the soap allowed to cool in the boiling pan with occasional stirring. At this point, perfume and colour can be stirred into the soap, if required, and the final soap poured into soap moulding boxes. It is then allowed to stay for 24-36 hours to harden, after which the moulds are emptied and the solid soap block cut into the required sizes and stamped.

6.2 Full-boiling Process

The process, popularly used by large and some small soap industries is the most important commercial method of soapmaking. It involves the treatment of fats or oils with an appropriate amount of alkali and removal of waste lye from the soap at the end of the process. The process produces hard and firm soaps, though it takes a longer time than the semi-boiling process, and is mostly used for the production of laundry soap and soap bases for toilet soaps.

The process consists of four stages, namely saponification of the oil with alkali, graining out of the soap, boiling on strength (or clear boiling) and fitting.

Plate 13: Soap-boiling using a TCC-designed boiling tank capable of producing 500 bars of soap a day

6.2.1 Saponification Process

The process is started by putting the melted oil into the boiling tank and running a weak (9-10%) caustic soda solution into the oil. The mixture is then boiled to start the saponification. The beginning of the saponification is denoted by the formation of an emulsion. When saponification has started caustic soda of higher strength (18°Bé solution of relative density 1·4) is frequently added in small quantities with continued boiling.

Sometimes it proves difficult to start the saponification and in such cases a small quantity of soap scrap may be added to induce the saponification. Rapid addition of caustic alkali in the initial stages can also entirely delay saponification in which case water should be added and the boiling continued till the excess alkali is taken up for the saponification to proceed. The end of saponification can be crudely determined by the 'ribbon' and 'taste' tests already discussed in Section 6.1.1. When

43

saponification is completed, the soap becomes firm and dry with a permanent faint caustic taste on the tongue when cooled. The soap, which now consists of imperfect soap together with water in which is dissolved glycerin and any slight excess of caustic soda, is then ready for graining out.

6.2.2 Graining Out

The object of this is to separate the waste lye (which is a mixture of glycerin produced during the soap boiling process and excess caustic soda solution) from the soap. This is brought about by the use of common salt in the dry form or as brine. The term 'graining' is used here because after the introduction of the salt, the homogeneous soap has the appearance of grains. During the graining process, brine of relative density 1·2 is added to the boiling soap and boiling is continued. Too much brine must not be added at a time. Usually the total salt used is 8-10% by weight of the oil used, depending on the type of oil. Less salt is required for tallow and palm oil while more salt is needed for coconut and palm kernel oils. As the salt is added and the soap allowed to boil and stirred, the soap is gradually thrown out of the solution, and loses its transparent and homogeneous appearance, becoming opaque and grainy. The graining is complete when the soap is practically free from foam and floats as neat soap on the lye. At this stage, a sample of soap taken from the tank consists of distinct grains of soap and a liquid portion which will easily separate. The boiling is then stopped and the excess lye allowed to settle for several hours or overnight.

It is necessary to cover the boiling pan and allow slow settling of the lye over a longer period of time to give the soap mass enough time to separate into four layers, namely, a small bottom layer of brine with impurities, and excess lye, a second layer of soap containing some salt and water, a third layer of clean transparent soap (neat soap), and a top layer of a thin crust of soap. The bottom layer of brine is drained out while the second and top layers can be removed and converted into bar soap by boiling with water.

The third layer of neat grainy soap is either worked out with a trowel to break the grains to obtain homogeneous soap, or boiled with a small quantity of water to bring it to a smooth homogeneous form and cooling after draining into soap moulds. When the soap is sufficiently cooled in the soap moulding box, it is taken from the mould, cut into the required sizes and stamped ready for use.

6.2.3 Clear Boiling and Fitting

The object of clear boiling and fitting is to obtain a pure soap suitable for the making of toilet soaps, by removing the last traces of impurities from the grained soap. In the clear boiling, complete saponification is attained and the soap is hardened. During the process, the bottom layer of the soap is drained out after the graining. The content of the boiling tank is then boiled with strong caustic solution of 25-30°Bé (relative density 1.21 to 1.26). More solution is added as it is absorbed until the soap is again grained, and is then allowed to boil steadily. As the boiling continues, complete saponification takes place, and the boiling is stopped. The grained soap is left for some hours to allow the settling of the excess lye which is then drained off.

The soap is then boiled with a little water to make it smooth and homogeneous. This boiling process is called 'fitting'. During the fitting operation, samples of the soap are taken from time to time to determine the quality of the soap and the end of the operation. If the soap is good, a small quantity taken on a trowel should slip off from it without adhering to its sides. If the soap adheres, too much heat was used for the fitting, and a little lye must therefore be carefully added to the soap and boiled again until the desired condition is attained, and the boiling stopped. After the fitting, the boiling pan is covered and allowed to stay for 2-6 days depending on the quality of soap in the pan. On complete settling, the content of the pan divides into four layers consisting of a top layer of a thin crust of soap, a second layer of good settled soap containing about 60-63% of total fatty matter (TFM), a third layer of darker soap with TFM of about 30%, forming about 15-20% of soap in the pan, and a bottom layer of spent lye containing glycerin and which can be extracted.

6.3 Treatment of Settled Soaps

After the soap has settled into the four layers the bottom layer of spent lye is drained off while the third and top layers are collected and converted into low grade soap by boiling. The second layer of good soap is then drained into another pan (i.e. cleansed) and treated to obtain the final product. In the cleansing process, care is taken to avoid the presence of any of the low grade soap forming the third layer. The temperature at which the soap is cleansed depends on the soap type — soaps to be 'liquored' should not be cleansed too hot or separation will take place during the liquoring; a temperature of 66°C is an ideal temperature for this. Cleansing temperatures of 74-76°C are suitable for firm unliquored soaps.

After the cleansing, the soap is stirred, or clutched, until a sufficiently low temperature is attained.

6.3.1 Liquoring
This involves the addition of various alkali solutions to the cleansed soap to produce soaps of different qualities. Liquoring can be done during the stirring (clutching). Among the alkalis most frequently used are sodium silicate and sodium carbonate. The latter may be used in the form of soda crystals containing 63% of water dissolved in its own water of crystallization on heating, and in that manner added, giving it firmness and increasing its detergent properties. It can also be added to soap as a solution of soda ash, either concentrated (of relative density 1·31) or of various strengths (of relative density 1·125 upwards) at a temperature of 60°C to stiffen and harden the soap.

In the choice of the solutions, care must be taken as strong soda ash solution in firm soaps results in a brittle product, whereas the texture of a weak soap will be greatly improved by such addition. It is advisable to have test samples of solutions in the soap to find out what proportions and strengths of sodium silicate or carbonate will be best suited to the grade of soap to be produced. However, 10% of the quantity of the soap is preferable.

6.3.2 Filling
This operation is done after the cleansing and clutching, or after the liquoring if the cleansed soap is liquored. The filling agents, as already described in Section 2.3 of Chapter 2 serve no useful purpose except that of increasing the bulk of the soap and hence adding weight to it. After choosing the right filler, the required quantity is stirred into the soap.

Plate 14: Draining semi-boiled soap from the boiling tank to the moulding box lined with polythene sheet

6.3.3 Framing

Having cleansed, clutched, liquored and filled the soap, the soap may be perfumed and drained into soap mouding boxes (frames) to solidify into blocks. The length of time the soap should be cooled is dependent on the quality and quantity of soap as well as the temperature of the surroundings. This time may vary from 3-7 days after which the soap blocks are removed from the frames, ready for cutting.

6.3.4 Drying and Stamping

After the soap has been cut into the required bars using a cutting table, bar soap can be dried by stacking the bars across each other so that air has free access to each bar for a day. They are then placed in storage bins for 2-3 weeks when they will be in perfect condition for packaging and distribution. Heavily liquored soaps are unsuitable for long periods of drying treatment, as the bars may tend to lose water rapidly,

Plate 15: Removing soap from the soap moulding box for cutting

Plate 16: Soap cutting operation. The soap block is first cut into slabs before being cut into bars

48

Plate 17: Arranging finished soap bars on shelves for drying

resulting in shrinkage and distortion. The dry soap is then stamped by means of a stamping machine. If necessary, the soap is transferred to racks after the stamping to expose it to air after which it is wrapped and put into cartons for the market.

6.4 Cold Process

This process involves the treatment of fat or oil with a definite amount of alkali and no separation of waste lye. Although it is possible with great care to produce neutral soap by this process the soap is very liable to contain both free alkali and unsaponified fat. The process is based on the fact that the glyceroles of certain low fatty acids oils (e.g. nut oils like) coconut and palm kernel oils) readily combine with strong caustic soda solutions at low temperatures, and generate sufficient heat to complete the saponification reaction.

Coconut oil is the chief oil employed but sometimes tallow, palm oil lard, cotton seed oil, or even castor oil can be blended with coconut or palm kernel oil to make the soap, with slight temperature change to render the blend liquid. Soaps made with these blends resemble, in appearance, milled toilet soaps.

In this process, it is very necessary to use high grade raw materials. Oils and fats should be free from excess acidity because caustic soda rapidly neutralizes free fatty acids forming granules of soap which grain out in the presence of strong caustic solution, and since the grainy soap is difficult to remove without heat increase, the soap tends to become thick and gritty and sometimes discolours. The caustic soda being used must also be pure, i.e. must contain as little carbonate as possible, and the water must be soft and all other materials carefully freed from particles of dirt.

The process involves stirring into the milled fat or oil in a tank, half its weight of caustic soda solution of 40°Bé of (relative density 1·37) at a temperature of 24°C for coconut and 38°C to 49°C for the blends. The running of the caustic solution into the oil must be done slowly and continuously. When the solution is being run into the oil the mixture must be stirred in one direction. When all the caustic soda solution has been run into the oil and the mixture stirred for 30-45 minutes, chemical reaction takes place with the generation of heat, finally resulting in the saponification of the oil. The content of the tank looks thin at first, but after some few hours it becomes a solid mass. The edges of the soap become more transparent as the process advances, and when the transparency has extended to the whole mass, the soap is ready, after perfuming to be poured into moulding boxes for hardening, cutting and stamping.

A little caustic potash solution used to blend the caustic soda solution greatly improves the appearance of the soap, making it smoother and milder.

If filling agents are to be incorporated in the soap this is done after the running in of the caustic solution. For laundry soaps, silicate of soda, talc and starch are chiefly used. Silicate solutions must be of strength 30°Tw. However, it is quite possible to make a soap of 45-50% TFM without any filling agent being added, simply by using a weaker caustic lye.

Some Advantages and Disadvantages of Cold Process over Boiling Process

Advantages

	Cold Process	Hot Process
i.	Requires inexpensive equipment and hence small capital investment.	Equipment and capital investment can be very expensive.
ii.	Less skilled labour, and simple processing technique.	More skilled and experienced labour required. Processing technique more complex.
iii.	Glycerin produced during the soap making process is retained in the soap, preventing the cracking of the soap on keeping, and increasing its emollient properties.	Glycerin removed (except for semi-boiling process).
iv.	Soap produced easily dissolves in water with abundant lather.	The soap is not readily soluble except when certain percentages of soft oils are used.
v.	Soap has whiter colour, and hence the process is used to produce some special types of soap.	Produces soaps of varying colours.
vi.	The process is quicker and requires inexpensive perfumes for scenting.	The process is long, sometimes taking weeks (full boiling) to complete.

Disadvantages

	Cold Process	Hot Process
i.	Bad soaps produced cannot be reclaimed using the same process.	Bad soaps produced can be reclaimed using the same process.
ii.	Soap normally contains slightly higher levels of free caustic alkali.	Process allows the production of neutral soaps.
iii.	Only small quantities of soap can be produced at a time.	Large quantities of soap can be produced at a time.
iv.	Process produces soap of less purity as impurities in spent lye cannot be washed.	Very pure soap can be produced during graining process.

Chapter 7

Small-scale Production of Toilet Soaps

By definition, a toilet soap is a soap specially adapted for toilet use due to its good detergent and lathering properties, as well as its freedom from caustic alkali and any other ingredient likely to cause irritation to the skin.

Toilet soaps can be classified according to their method of manufacture into the following classes:
a) cold process soap,
b) milled soap,
c) remelted soap.

The processes for the manufacturing of these three types of soaps are described below.

7.1 Cold Process

In practice, good toilet soaps are produced using the milling method. However, on the small scale, some of the relatively cheaper varieties of toilet soaps can be made using the cold process.

The manufacturing technique is almost the same as already described in Section 6.4. The process consists of melting the fat or oil in a pan and sieving out any impurities in it, after settling. The oil is then run into the saponifying pan and cooled to 35°C. The right quantities of dye and perfume are then stirred into the oil. Dyestuff should be dissolved in a small quantity of water and filtered to avoid specks of colour in the soap. For carbolic varieties, the cresylic acid is not added until after the saponification of the oil. After adding the dye and perfume to the oil the required quantity and strength (38-40°Bé) of caustic soda solution is run into it in a thin stream with constant stirring until the oil is completely saponified and the mass begins to thicken. Finally the thickened mass is drained into soap moulding boxes and allowed to harden slowly.

The quantities of raw materials to be used depend on the type of soap to be produced. For simple white toilet soaps for example, a blend of oils consisting of 20kg of coconut oil, 27·3kg of tallow (or palm oil) and 1·8kg of castor oil is treated with 25kg of 40°Bé caustic soda solution.

7.2 Milled Toilet Soapmaking

Almost all the high class soaps used on the market pass through the milling process which consists briefly of the following operations: drying of soap base, mixing of perfume and dye, milling, compressing, cutting and stamping.

7.2.1 Drying of Soap Base

The final soap obtained after the treatment of the settled soap already described in Section 6.3 serves as a soap base for the milled soap. After the solidification in soap frames, this soap contains 28-30% of water, and this quantity has to be reduced by half before any satisfactory milling can be done. Drying is best done by chipping the soap into smaller sizes and exposing the chips in trays to a current of hot air at 35-40°C. There are several forms of drying chambers in which the chips in the trays are placed upon a series of racks, one above the other and warm air circulated through.

It is very important that the correct amount of moisture should be left in the soap, not too much or little — the exact point can be determined only by judgement and experience, and depends on the nature of the soap to be made and the quantity of perfume to be added. However, a range of 11-14% moisture gives good results. Below this range, the soap will crumble during the milling process and the finished soap will have the tendency to crack, while above the range, the soap will stick to the rollers of the milling machine, and mill only with difficulty.

7.2.2 Mixing of Perfume and Dye

When the soap chips have been dried to attain the required water content, they are put into the amalgamator (the mixing machine) and the required amount of perfume and dye added to mix thoroughly at toom temperature.

The quantity of perfume to be added varies considerably with the perfume type. For cheap grade soaps 0·6 to 1·7% (by weight of soap) are used, while for costly soaps 2-3% are sometimes used.

7.2.3 Milling

From the amalgamator, the soap is put into the milling machine for the chips to be milled into more homogeneous thin soap ribbons. Prolonged milling does not improve the quality of the soap but only gives a semi-transparent appearance to it.

7.2.4 Compressing

This follows the milling process. The operation tends to bind the soap ribbons into a solid bar suitable for cutting and stamping. In this process, the milled soap is fed into the compressor (or plodder), and as the compression takes place the soap extrudes through the nozzle of the compressor as a long polished solid bar.

7.24 Cutting and Stamping

In cutting the extruded soap into the required sizes for stamping, the cutter should shape it somewhat similar to the required finished tablets. An ordinary cutting table can be employed. Stamping of the cut pieces can be done with either foot or hand operated stamping machines.

7.3 Remelted Soaps

In this method of making low grade toilet soaps, a mixture of various kinds of soaps is remelted in a boiling pan and stirred. The stirring or agitation should not be too vigorous or lengthy as this will cause the soap to become aerated. When all the soap is melted, addition of peal ash (potassium carbonate) solution is made to the soap to give it a firmer and smoother texture, render it more transparent and increase its lathering properties. The required colour is then added in a soluble form, and lastly the perfume. To give the desired odour, large quantities of perfume need to be added; hence cheaper essential oils should be used.

The perfumed soap is then drained into frames for cooling, cutting and stamping.

Chapter 8

Non-edible Oils for Soapmaking

Traditionally, soapmaking in Ghana and many other African countries involves the use of various types of edible oils and fats. However, over the years there has been a very rapid increase in the demand for edible oils and fats for both consumption and industrial purposes. This has resulted in the increase in the price of such edible oils like palm, coconut, palm kernel and shea butter which are extensively used in Ghana for soapmaking. The large increase in the prices of edible oils has in turn rendered soapmaking relatively unprofitable. It has therefore become imperative to search for other alternative sources of raw materials which could provide suitable substitutes for the edible oils traditionally employed in soapmaking.

In Ghana some research on the use of non-edible oils for soapmaking, carried out by the Technology Consultancy Centre, has identified three locally available plants whose oil seeds produce non-edible oils which can be used for the production of soap. These three are neem, castor and physic nut *(Jatropha).*

8.1 Neem Oil

Neem oil is obtained from the seeds of the neem tree. In Ghana, apart from the trees being planted in cities for shade, they are also cultivated on plantations by the Forestry Department for use as firewood. Such plantations are found in the Accra Plains, Achimota, Winneba, Navrongo, Yendi, Bawku, Cape Coast and Inchaban.

The oil content of the local kernel is about 45%, and the oil is greenish yellow, non-drying with an acrid and bitter taste,

Plate 18: A neem tree branch with fruits

and an unpleasant garlic odour. The oil is extensively used to blend other oils in the making of both laundry and toilet soaps in India. Analysis of locally extracted oil gave the following properties.

Physical Properties

Colour	greenish yellow
Odour	repulsive garlic
Taste	very bitter
Solubility	insoluble in water
Density	0.905g/cc
Refractive Index	1.47

Chemical Properties

Saponification Value	194.78
Iodine Value	65
Unsaponifiable matter	2.5%

8.1.1 Soapmaking Properties

The oil saponifies readily and gives a hard-grained soap with good and very stable lather. When used alone for the making of soap it is very necessary to grain the soap as this helps to remove most of the disagreeable odour and colour. On the other hand, if it is used to make soap with other oils, it is advisable to first make neem oil soap. After the soap has been grained, the other oils are stirred into the soap and the required amount of caustic soda solution added to start the saponification again. Neem oil soap is used for both laundry and antiseptic purposes.

Below is the analytical results of neem oil soap made from local neem oil.

Analysis of Neem Oil Soap

	Analysis Result	
Property	*Hot Process Soap*	*Cold Process Soap*
Odour	Slightly garlic	Garlic
Lather stability	Much lather and stable over long periods	Much lather and stable over long periods
Hardness	hard	hard
Washing Efficiency	high	high
Total Fatty Matter	70.4%	60%
Free Caustic Alkali	0.0%	0.1%
Moisture	20.1%	25.2%

8.2 Castor Oil

Castor oil is obtained from the seeds of the castor plant (*Abonkruma* in Fanti). In Ghana, the oil has no economic value as no oil is extracted from the seeds. Apart from using the plant to give shade to young seedlings of oil palm, cocoa, coffee and coconut at nurseries of the Ministry of Agriculture, the plants are normally seen growing wild, especially at the outskirts of towns and villages in both savanna and forest zones of Ghana.

Plate 19: Castor plant

The seed contains 45-55% of oil which can be used to blend other oils for soapmaking. Below are the properties of locally extracted castor oil.

Physical Properties

Colour	—	Light yellow or colourless
Odour	—	acrid
Taste	—	nauseating
Relative density	—	0.93

Chemical Properties

Saponification Value	184
Iodine Value	83.6

Soapmaking Properties

Castor oil consists mainly of ricinoeic acid and smaller percentages of stearic and palmitic acids. The oil has the same behaviour as coconut oil as regards to saponification, being readily saponified with strong caustic lye. The oil produces hard, white, and transparent soap. Below are the analyzed properties of soap made from locally extracted castor oil.

Analysis of Castor Oil Soap

Property	Analysis result of soap (Hot process)
Colour	pale
Hardness	very hard
Lather stability	much lather but very unstable — lather vanishes after few seconds
Washing efficiency	low
Total fatty matter	67%
Free caustic alkali	0.0%
Moisture	20.5%

8.3 Physic Oil

The physic oil is obtained from the seeds of the physic nut (or *Jatropha*) plant, locally called *Adaadze* in Fanti or *Nktandua* in Twi. The plant is often grown for hedges and fences but commonly found growing wild around the Afram plains, central region around Cape Coast, and the Axim area. The seed contains about 52% oil. The oil has been used along with plantain ashes for the making of home-made soaps in Ghana in the olden days. However, its use in the production of soap has been forgotten in recent times.

Locally, the oil has been found to have the following properties:

Colour	Colourless
Relative Density	0.91
Refractive Index	1.47
Saponification Value	—
Iodine Value	78.3

8.3.1 Soapmaking Properties

Physic oil soap is relatively soft but produces a lot of very stable lather over long period of time. To increase its hardness the oil can be blended with 10-20% of castor oil.

PLATE 20: Physic Nut Plant with Fruits.

8.4 Process of Soapmaking

Due to the complexity of the full boiling process, it is generally not used in small and village scale soapmaking. However, the semi-boiling and the cold process normally used by the small-scale soapmakers are not suitable for use with non-edible oils due to the fact that majority of these oils have deep colour and bad odour. Instead, a combination of the full-boiling and semi-boiling process is used.

In the combined process, the deep coloured and bad smelling non-edible oils to be purified are first saponified, and then grained to remove the colour and odour. The grained soap obtained is used in soapmaking together with other pale coloured oils, using the semi-boiled process.

A typical formulation and process involving the use of neem, castor and physic nut oils is described as follows:

Raw Materials

Neem oil	60kg
Physic nut oil	35kg
Castor oil	5kg
Caustic soda	14kg
Sodium Carbonate	25kg
Common Salt	8kg

Process

The neem oil is clarified by boiling with an equal volume of water and draining the water out after settling, with the dirt from the oil. 8·4kg of the caustic soda is then dissolved in 25kg of water to form a 33% solution. The neem oil is then put in a boiling pan over fire and the caustic solution run into it little by little with proper stirring. When all the caustic soda is used up in the saponification of the oil after about 4-5 hours boiling, the salt is dissolved in a small quantity of water and is added to the soap and stirred. The homogeneous soap is then grained and the colouring matter in the oil separates out from the soap and settles down with the excess lye. About 80kg of water is then added to the grained soap and after proper stirring for some time, the contents of the boiling pan are allowed to settle for one night, when the pure soap floats on the surface of the lye. The coloured spent lye with the impurities are drained out, and the soap melted with some quantity of water.

It must be noted that since non-edible oils have comparatively large proportions of free fatty acids, retardation of the saponification sometimes occurs because the free fatty acids sometimes form granular soap and accumulate a considerable quantity of caustic soda, thus preventing free contact between the oil and the caustic. When retardation occurs some water should be added to the soap and boiled with stirring.

The melted neem soap can be drained into soap moulding boxes to harden and keep for future use, or when a continuous process is being done, the neem soap is melted with some water. Meanwhile the remaining 6·6kg of caustic soda is dissolved in 16·8kg of water. Some of the caustic solution is added to the melted soap and the physic nut and castor oils added and stirred. The remaning caustic solution is added to the soap in bits until it is all used up to complete the saponification process. The sodium carbonate (or 25kg of 40°Bé sodium silicate solution) can be introduced at this stage and stirred for about an hour. Colour and perfume may be added and the soap drained into moulding boxes. The temperature at the time of moulding, in the case of pure soap, should not exceed 70°C.

Chapter 9

Ghana Standards Specifications for Soap

There are certain international quality standards to which soaps, whether for laundry, toilet or medical purposes, have to conform before they are sent to the market. As a check on these standards it is necessary that samples of soap batches coming to the market from the manufacturer are physically and chemically analyzed.

In Ghana, the National Standard Board has promulgated certain standards for different types of soap (based on the British and Indian standards for soaps). Soaps produced commercially at both the large- and small-scale levels should satisfy these standards before they can be marketed under the Ghana Standard Board Certificate for soaps.

9.1 Filled Hard Soap Specifications

These soaps are defined as hard soaps containing fillers. They may be white or coloured, and should be well saponified, and in addition contain fillers.

Requirements

Generally, the soap should consist of alkali salts of fatty acids; it should be of firm texture, free from objectionable odour and have good lathering properties. It should either be in a form of a bar, ball, or tablet. The ingredient of the soap should be non-toxic. The soap shall also comply with the following specific chemical requirements.

Total fatty matter (% by mass)	Not less than 46
Free caustic alkali (% by mass)	Not greater than 0.05
Total free fat (% by mass)	Not greater than 0.2
Total free alkali as Na_2O (% by mass)	Not greater than 0.3
Moisture (% by mass)	Not greater than 30

63

9.2 Genuine Hard Soap Specification

This is defined as hard soap of a firm texture without the addition of any filler.

Physical Requirements
The soap should consist principally of the alkali salts of fatty acids, and be free from objectionable odour, and with good lathering properties. It should be in the form of a neat bar, ball, or tablet.

Chemical Requirements
It should be in addition to the above physical requirements have the following composition.

Total fatty matter	Not less than 59%
Free caustic alkali	Not more than 0.05%
Total caustic alkali	Not more than 0.2%
Total free alkali	Not more than 0.25%
Moisure	Not more than 28%

9.3 Filled Carbolic Soap Specifications

This is defined as hard soap containing fillers and phenolic substances like cresylic acid. Physically, the soap should be of firm texture, free from objectionable odour, and possess good lathering properties. The ingredient of the soap should be non-toxic. It may be in a form of a bar, tablet or ball.

Chemical Requirements

Total fatty matter	Not less than 46%
Free caustic alkali	Not greater than 0.05%
Total free fat	Not greater than 0.2%
Phenol content	Between 0.5-1.0%
Total free alkali as Na_2O	Not greater than 0.3%
Moisture	Not greater than 30%

9.4 Toilet Soap Specification

This is, by definition, soap meant for body washing other than genuine hard soap, carbolic soap, filled soap and medicated soap.

Physical Requirements
The soap shall consist principally of alkali salts of fatty acids; it should be of firm texture, free from objectionable odour, and

possess good lathering properties. The ingredient of the soap should be non-toxic.

Chemical Requirement
In addition to the above physical requirements, the soap should have the following chemical properties:

Total fatty matter	Not less than 75.6%
Free caustic alkali	Not more than 0.05%
Total free alkali	Not more than 0.22%
Moisture	Not more than 14%

9.5 Medicated Soap

This is defined as any soap other than carbolic soap for which therapeutic claims are made. The level of active ingredient must be indicated and must comply with the requirement of the code of good manufacturing practice for the Cosmetic and Toiletry Industry in Ghana.

The soap should consist principally of the alkali salts of fatty acids, be of firm texture, and free from objectionable odour. It should possess good lathering properties, and its ingredients should be non-toxic.

Chemical Requirements

	% by mass of soap
Total fatty matter	Not less than 63
Free caustic alkali	Not more than 0.05
Total free alkali	Not more than 0.25
Total free fat	Not more than 0.2
Matter insoluble in ethanol	Not more than 2.0
Chlorides	Not more than 0.8

9.6 Packaging and Marking of Soaps

Packaging. Soaps should be packaged in a suitable container made of a material that is not affected by soap.

Marking. The unwrapped soap should be clearly marked with the registered trade mark of the manufacturer. The container should be clearly marked with the following.
a) manufacturer's name and address, and registered trade mark
b) works indicating the type of soap
c) batch coding or lot identification number
d) minimum net weight (mass)
e) country of manufacture

f) Ghana Standard (GS) number
g) Ghana Standard Board Certificate Mark
h) In the case of medicated soap, there should be a conspicuous
   warning of the following nature

      i)   that use of the soap he discontinued immediately skin
   irritations or any other adverse reaction appears.

     ii)   that prolonged use may be dangerous.

In addition, for medicated soaps containing mercuric oxide the product should not be used on damaged skins, e.g. cut or open skin. This warning must appear on the outer cover of the container.

Appendix 1

Some typical formulations for soaps

1. Laundry soap — using semi-boiling process

Palm oil	150kg
Coconut oil	30kg
Caustic soda	28kg
Kaolin	15kg

2. Soft potassium soap (indigenous soap) — using semi-boiling process

Palm oil	22.5kg
Caustic potash	4.5kg (dissolved in 11.25kg of water)
Salt	440g

3. Laundry soap — using full boiling process

Palm oil	150kg
Coconut oil	30kg
Caustic soda	36.4kg
Kaolin	6.8kg
Salt	16.4kg

4. Carbolic soap — using full boiling process

Palm oil	180kg
Caustic soda	36.4kg
Kaolin	6.8kg
Salt	16.36kg
Sodium carbonate	1.36kg
Cresylic acid	6.8kg

5. Laundry soap — using cold process

a. Palm oil   16.4kg
   Coconut oil   2.2kg
   Caustic soda   3kg (dissolved in 7kg of water)

b. Palm oil   4.5kg
   Palm kernel oil   1.3kg
   Caustic soda   1kg (dissolved in 4.5kg of water)

6. Toilet soap — using cold process

a. Coconut oil   42.7kg
   Castor oil   3.7kg
   Caustic lye (38°Bé)   23kg

b Coconut oil   22.7kg
   Tallow (or Palm oil)   22.7kg
   Caustic lye (37°Bé)   22.7kg

7. Transparent soap — using semi-boiling process

a. Coconut oil   1.8kg
   Caustic soda   1.2kg (dissolved in water to obtain a 20°Bé solution)

Note: The method involves the production of soap stock using the above raw materials. The stock is then dried to 30-35°C. The next operation involves dissolving 50 parts of the dried soap in 50 parts of the industrial methylated spirit on moderate heat, and cooling in frames. It must be noted that the transparency of the soap is found after it has been exposed to dry air for a considerable period.

8. Liquid soap — semi-boiling process

   Coconut oil   182kg
   50°Bé Caustic potash
      solution   100kg
   Additional water   135 litres

Note: The method involves heating the coconut oil to 50°C and running the caustic solution and water in and stirring; saponification takes place and the resultant soap is a 50-55% soap which is then diluted with hot softened water to obtain the desired concentration.

9. Hand protective cream for mechanics

This type of soap has wide sales throughout paint, auto-accessory, hardware and drug stores. It is applied to hands and arms so as to form a barrier to paint, grease, etc while working.

Formula

88-92% soap chips	5.45kg
Water	32.7kg
Mineral oil or lanolin	2.2kg
N-Brand Sodium Silicate	4.45kg

Method

The soap is dissolved in hot water. The silicate is added and the mass is mixed and cooled. The mineral oil and 112gm of perfume are admixed, with stirring until uniform. The product may be filled into cans.

Appendix 2

Properties of soaps from different oils/fats

Oil	Texture	Lathering Property	Cleaning Property	Effect on Skin	Uses
Neem	fairly soft	More and stable lather	Good	Antiseptic	washing, bathing and medicinal
Coconut	very hard	Plenty and fairly stable lather	very good	No effect	washing, bathing and shaving
Tallow	hard	More and stable lathe	very good	No effect	washing, bathing and shaving
Palm oil	hard	More and stable lather	very good	No effect	washing and bathing
Palm kernel	very hard	Plenty and fairly stable lather	good	No effect	washing and bathing
Groundnut	soft	Less and stable lather	very good	No effect	washing and bathing
Shea butter	fairly hard	Fairly good lather	good	No effect	washing and bathing
Cocoa butter	hard	Good lather	good	No effect	washing and bathing